STRANGE BUT TRUE

Gross Anatomy

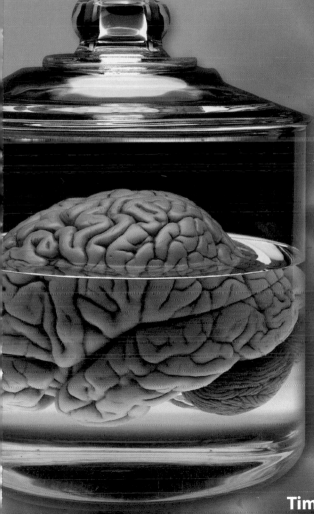

Timothy J. Bradley

Consultants

Timothy Rasinski, Ph.D.
Kent State University

Lori Oczkus
Literacy Consultant

Dana Lambrose,
M.S.N., P.M.H.N.P.
West Coast University

Based on writing from
TIME For Kids. *TIME For Kids* and the *TIME For Kids* logo are registered trademarks of TIME Inc. Used under license.

Publishing Credits

Dona Herweck Rice, *Editor-in-Chief*
Lee Aucoin, *Creative Director*
Jamey Acosta, *Senior Editor*
Lexa Hoang, *Designer*
Stephanie Reid, *Photo Editor*
Rane Anderson, *Contributing Author*
Rachelle Cracchiolo, *M.S.Ed., Publisher*

Image Credits: cover, p.1 Alamy; p.10 Corbis; p.31 Getty Images/Ikon Images; p.9 (top) National Geographic Stock; p.15 (top) AFP/Getty Images/Newscom; p.23 (bottom right) EPA/Newscom; p.9 (bottom) imago stock&people/Newscom; p.16 Reuters/Newscom; pp.10, 19 (top) Photo Researchers, Inc.; pp.8, 12–13, 15 (bottom), 19 (bottom), 21, 25, 28–29, 38–39 John Scahill; All other images from Shutterstock.

Teacher Created Materials

5301 Oceanus Drive
Huntington Beach, CA 92649-1030
http://www.tcmpub.com
ISBN 978-1-4333-4860-0
© 2013 Teacher Created Materials, Inc.
Made in China
Nordica.112016.CA21601787

Table of Contents

Bizarre Biology 4

Bones and Muscles 6

Skin 14

Respiration and Circulation 18

Digestion .24

The Five Senses 30

The Brain 36

Human Body 2.0 40

Glossary .42

Index 44

Bibliography 46

More to Explore 47

About the Author 48

Bizarre Biology

There's a lot more than just blood and guts inside the human body. There's gas, earwax, vomit, scabs, pus, boogers, and belches, too! From head to toe, our bodies are amazing—and gross!

Around 2,000 years ago, scientists began to peek inside. They began to **dissect** human bodies. From the outside, we may look pretty boring. But cut us open, and inside you'll find a world stranger than any planet.

Anatomy 101

Human anatomy is the part of science that deals with our body's structure. The words *gross anatomy* don't refer to parts of the body that are gross. They refer to parts of the body that can be studied with the human eye—no microscope required!

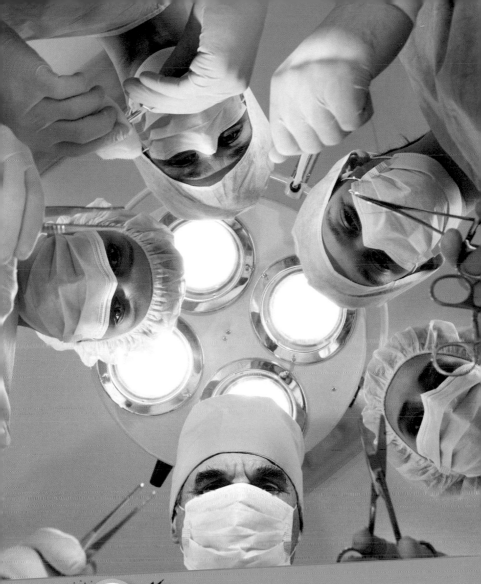

THINK LINK

1 What lies below our skin?

2 How do the different parts of the body work together?

3 How would our lives change if our bodies were different?

Bones and Muscles

What would happen if your bones and muscles suddenly disappeared? You would flop to the ground, unable to move or function. You would be a puddle of skin, blood, and guts. The only good news is you wouldn't be able to live very long in this state.

All animals need a stable frame to move around. The **organs** inside our bodies need to be protected. Fish, amphibians, birds, and mammals all have an internal skeleton. The skeleton supports the organs and protects the brain. The human skeleton is made of bone. A strong internal skeleton supports the body. It lets us do things like ride skateboards and climb trees.

Muscles and bones work together to support the body.

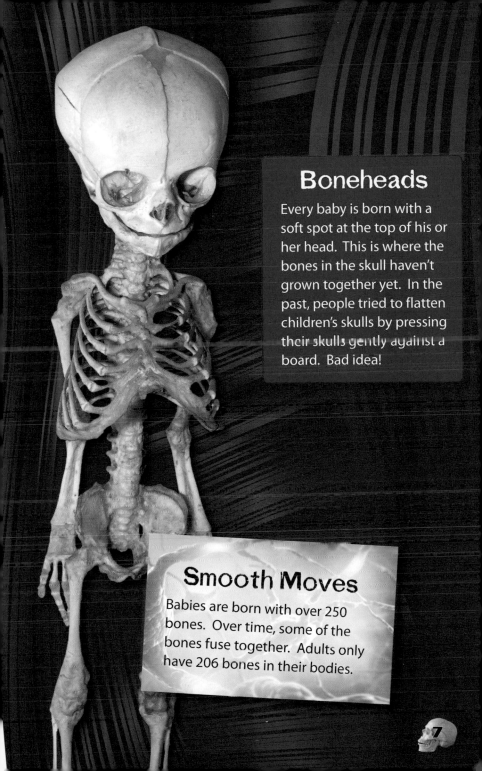

Boneheads

Every baby is born with a soft spot at the top of his or her head. This is where the bones in the skull haven't grown together yet. In the past, people tried to flatten children's skulls by pressing their skulls gently against a board. Bad idea!

Smooth Moves

Babies are born with over 250 bones. Over time, some of the bones fuse together. Adults only have 206 bones in their bodies.

No bones about it. Our skeletons hold us together. When you think of bones, you may picture the dry, hard bones you see in a museum. But our bones are alive. They grow and change just like the rest of the body. If a bone is broken, the body is able to repair it. New bone joins the broken ends, and the repaired bone may be as strong as it was before.

Bone is made of **calcium** and other elements. Calcium is very strong. **Ligaments** and **tendons** hold the bones together. Joints are formed where the bones meet. The elbow is one of the most used joints in the body. To keep the bones from rubbing against each other, pads of **cartilage** (KAR-tl-ij) cushion the joints. Throughout the day, cartilage shrinks. That's why we're taller in the morning and shorter at night!

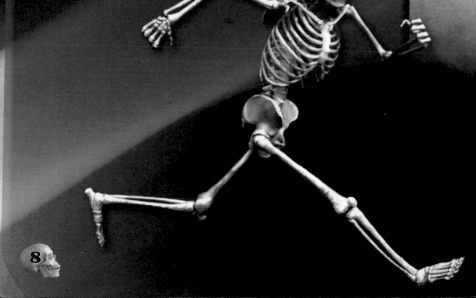

Foot Binding

For generations, many Chinese girls had their feet bound. Their toes were broken, tucked under, and then bandaged. Repeated bindings prevented the feet from growing to full size. Women with these tiny feet were admired. Some wore shoes as small as three inches. Today, foot binding is illegal.

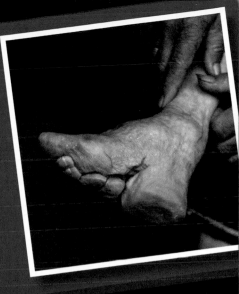

Beautiful Bones

The Padaung people in Thailand are famous for their long necks. Padaung women wear metal rings on their necks. Over time, these rings push down the collarbone and rib bones in the chest. This gives the illusion of a very long neck, which is believed to be beautiful.

Muscles

Muscles make it possible for the human body to move. They help us lift boxes, talk, and digest food. **Skeletal muscles** are the muscles most people are thinking of when they say *muscle*. They are tied to the skeleton with tendons and ligaments. **Smooth muscle** is used in **peristalsis** (per-uh-STAWL-sis) to push food through the body (down if you're lucky, up if you're not). **Cardiac muscle** never needs to rest like skeletal muscle does. The only time your heart rests is in between beats.

The heart may be the most important muscle in the body. But **sphincter** (SFINGK-ter) **muscles** are a close second. A sphincter is a ring-shaped smooth muscle. It opens and closes important areas of the body. One sphincter holds the food inside the stomach until it is ready to move on. Other sphincters hold waste in the body until it's time to go to the bathroom. A sphincter in the eye shrinks the pupil in bright light.

Little Hercules

Richard Sandrak is known as Little Hercules. When he was young, he started training for body-building and martial-arts competitions. At 8 years old, weighing 80 pounds, he could bench-press more than twice his own weight—that's over 150 pounds! Just remember, lifting too much weight when your bones and muscles are still growing can be dangerous. Talk to your doctor or PE teacher before starting any weight-lifting program.

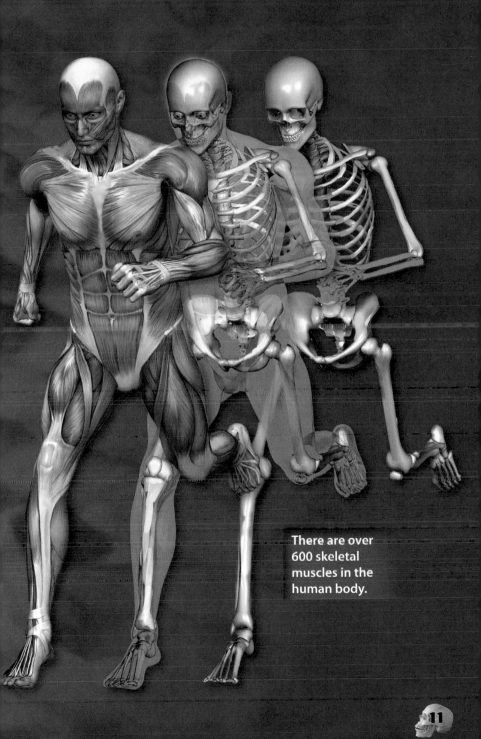

There are over 600 skeletal muscles in the human body.

Bones and Muscles

Doctors study **cadavers** to learn about what's under the skin. As they dissect the body, they discover how the different parts of the body work together. The skeleton lies at the center of each part, holding the body up. The muscles connect many different areas of the body.

It used to be common for anatomy students to write messages on the table under the cadaver. One student wrote, "His time was bad, but ours is worse."

Today, people allow their bodies to be studied after they die. But 200 years ago, people didn't want to donate their bodies. Body snatchers stole dead bodies from fresh graves. Then, they sold the bodies to anatomy schools. One body snatcher's punishment included a public dissection of his body!

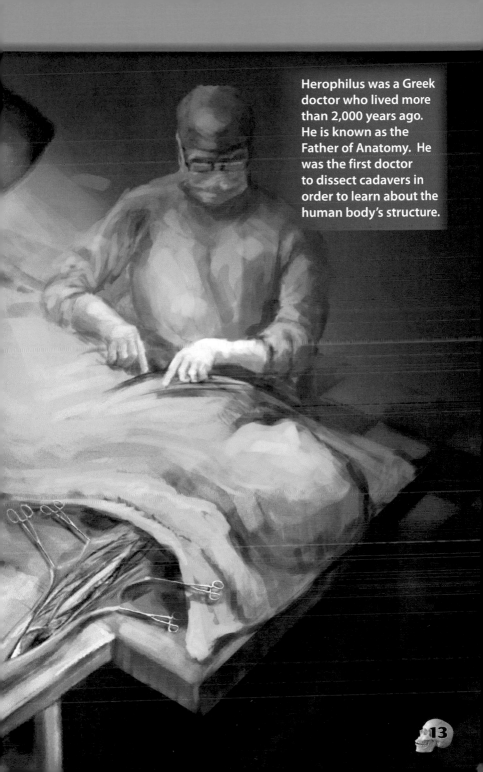

Herophilus was a Greek doctor who lived more than 2,000 years ago. He is known as the Father of Anatomy. He was the first doctor to dissect cadavers in order to learn about the human body's structure.

13

Skin

Skin cells work together to form the largest organ in the body. The skin acts as a giant shield against disease. Every scab and scar is a sign of the hard work skin does. Your skin protects your body from millions of **microorganisms**, including **bacteria**. Three million sweat **glands** in your skin help the body stay cool. We feel heat, pressure, and pain through our skin. And let's face it, skin makes us a little easier to look at!

Skin Planet

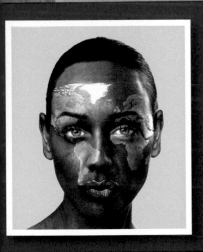

Think of your skin as a planet. The kind of bacteria that exists between the eyebrows is different from the kind found on the tip of the nose. Some areas of the skin are dry. Other areas are filled with oil. Just as some animals can survive in harsh places like the desert, only some bacteria do well on dry areas of skin. Others will only survive on oily patches.

Skin Twins

Can you imagine sharing your skin with someone else? Conjoined twins share skin as well as other organs. Some conjoined twins are attached at the head. Others are attached at lower points in the body. Doctors are finding ways to separate these twins so each can live his or her own healthy life.

Layers of Skin

The skin is made up of three layers.

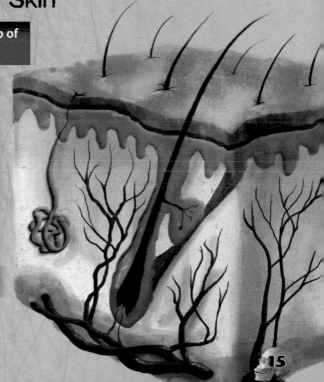

epidermis

dermis

subcutaneous tissue

Face Transplants

In a face transplant, facial tissue from a recently **deceased** person is sewn onto a patient with serious injuries. If the surgery goes well, the patient may be able to breathe and speak more clearly. In time, he or she may even show facial expressions again. The first face transplant was done in 2010.

Before

After

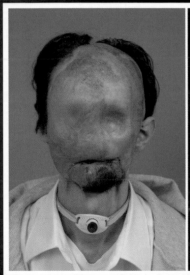

Dallas Wiens's face was severely burned by a live electrical wire. He was the first person in the United States to have a full face transplant.

Wiens was inspired to recover by his young daughter.

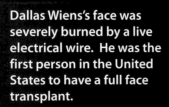

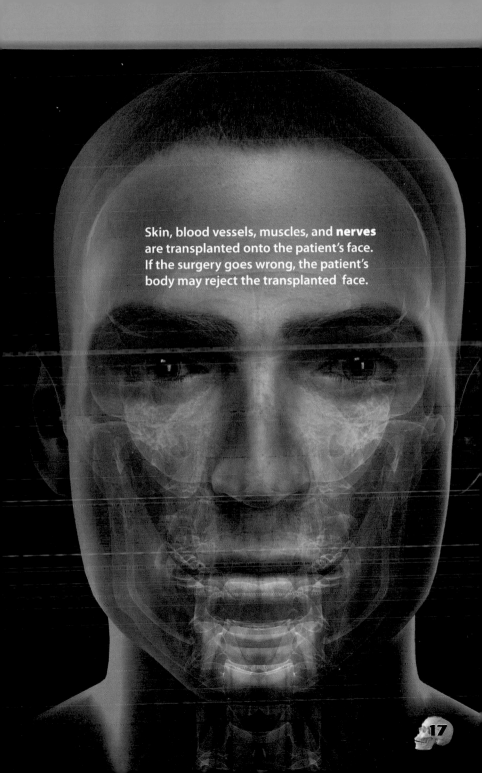

Skin, blood vessels, muscles, and **nerves** are transplanted onto the patient's face. If the surgery goes wrong, the patient's body may reject the transplanted face.

Respiration and Circulation

One breath in, one breath out. **Respiration**, or breathing, seems like a simple process. We do it without thinking. Whether we're singing, walking, running, or just thinking, we're breathing.

First, **oxygen** enters through the nose or mouth. The oxygen flows into the lungs and passes into the blood. Cells deliver waste back to the lungs. **Carbon dioxide** leaves the body on the exhale. This simple cycle is what keeps us alive.

Gulp!

Swimmers practice holding their breath so they can stay under water longer. Ricardo da Gama Bahia is the world record holder. He held his breath for over 20 minutes. The only way to do this is with medical help. Da Gama Bahia inhaled pure oxygen for 20 minutes before his attempt.

There He Blows!

A cough happens when the lungs push air quickly and forcefully out of the mouth. Thousands of small saliva droplets fly in a single cough. Some of those droplets can fly at up to 60 miles per hour!

The lungs are filled with air sacs that absorb and release oxygen.

Red blood cells pick up and drop off oxygen.

Circulation

The **circulatory system** is the highway of the body. Red blood cells act like dump trucks in a city. They carry oxygen and **nutrients** to all the organs in the body. The heart sets the pace. Fresh oxygenated blood moves from the lungs to the heart, where it is sent around the body. Blood cells carry oxygen throughout the body. Then, they come back to the heart and lungs to drop off carbon dioxide. It's time to pick up more oxygen.

Blood Bath

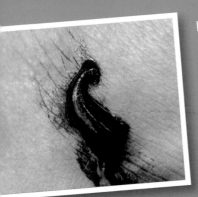

In the past, doctors often didn't know how to treat people who were sick or in pain. They believed that bleeding could cure the patient because it let the illness out. Leeches were often used for this process. Unfortunately, it usually only made patients weaker. Extreme bleeding, or **bloodletting**, can be a painful and slow way to die.

The human heart can pump five liters of blood around the body in just one minute.

The Human Heart

The right and left sides of the heart are labeled in this diagram as though the heart was looking out from the body.

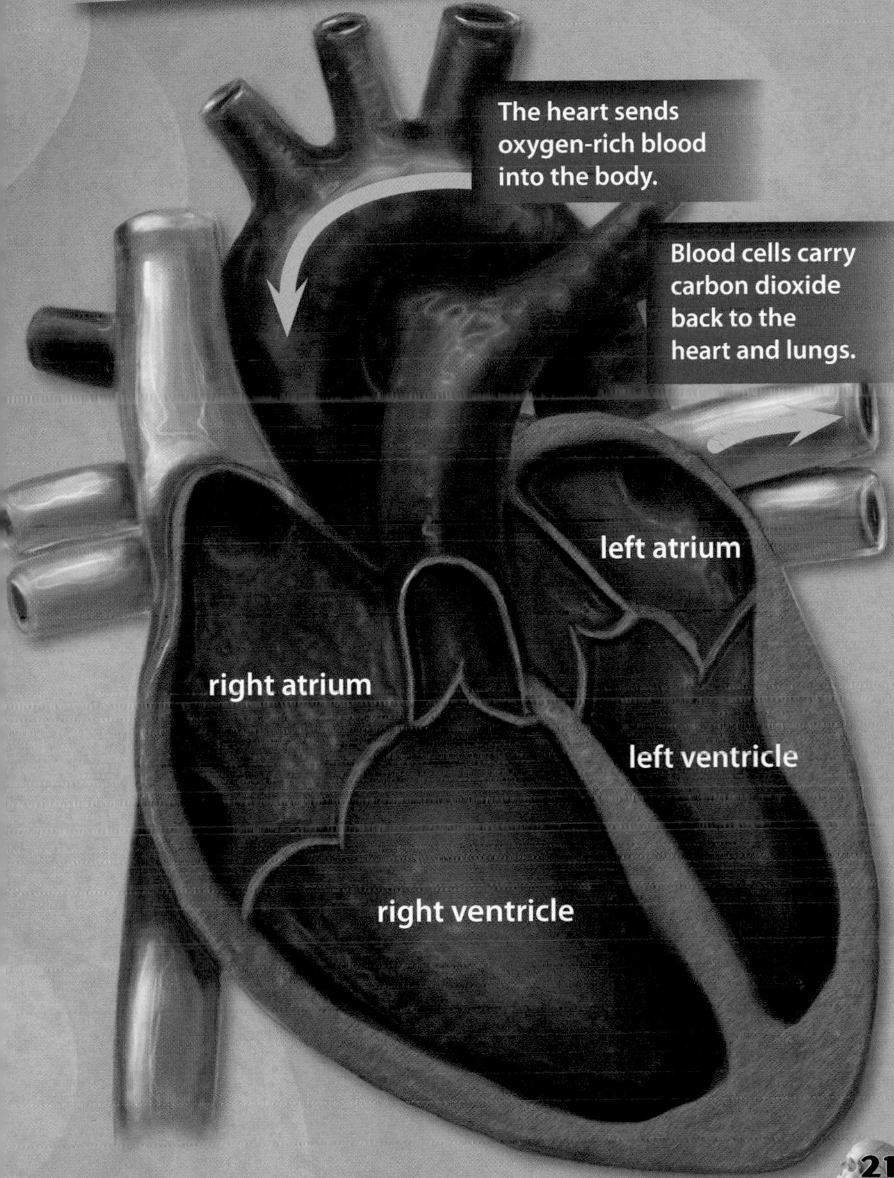

The heart sends oxygen-rich blood into the body.

Blood cells carry carbon dioxide back to the heart and lungs.

left atrium

right atrium

left ventricle

right ventricle

Red Gold

Blood is known as *red gold* because it is so valuable. We can't live without it. In the United States, patients need blood transfusions every two seconds. They need blood from someone else to survive. They may be sick, or they may have lost blood in surgery or an accident. Thousands of people donate blood every year. Their blood is used in transfusions to save lives. Here's what happens.

1 A healthy person donates a pint of blood. Donors must be at least 17 years old to donate. Donating blood takes about an hour.

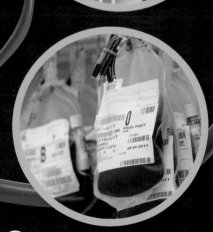

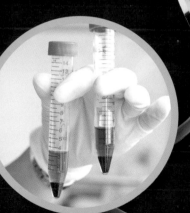

2 The blood is tested and processed. The different parts of the blood are separated. A single donation can save three lives.

3 Each unit of blood is assigned a code. This helps doctors track the blood and make sure it stays safe.

STOP! THINK...

• Why do you think only 10 percent of people donate blood?

• What other names would you use to describe blood?

• What do you think is the most important step in this process?

4 Blood is sent to hospitals around the country. Stored in refrigerators, the blood is safe from disease.

5 When a patient needs blood, a transfusion is given. Donated blood is pumped into the patient. In time, the patient may one day grow strong enough to donate blood as well.

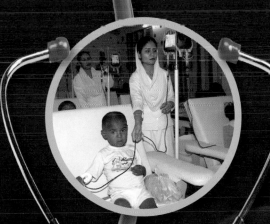

Digestion

The food you eat and drink gives your body energy. Your **digestive system** takes in nutrients from food. These nutrients travel on through the circulatory system to reach the rest of the body. It's a long journey, but it's worth it. These nutrients keep your body healthy, help it grow, and give you the energy to work and play.

Along the way, it can be a messy ride from food to poop! A normal meal can cause burps, gas, and ferociously bad breath. And a bad meal can come up in the form of vomit!

I'm Stuffed

The large intestine is about five feet long! It is coiled up so it can fit inside your body.

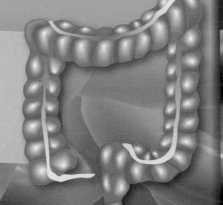

How Food Becomes Poop

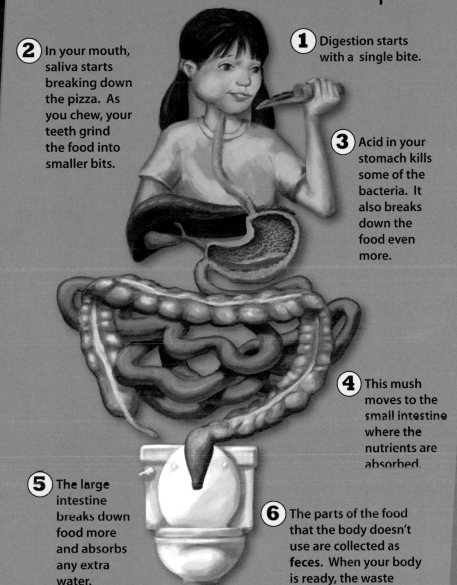

2 In your mouth, saliva starts breaking down the pizza. As you chew, your teeth grind the food into smaller bits.

1 Digestion starts with a single bite.

3 Acid in your stomach kills some of the bacteria. It also breaks down the food even more.

4 This mush moves to the small intestine where the nutrients are absorbed.

5 The large intestine breaks down food more and absorbs any extra water.

6 The parts of the food that the body doesn't use are collected as **feces**. When your body is ready, the waste comes out as poop!

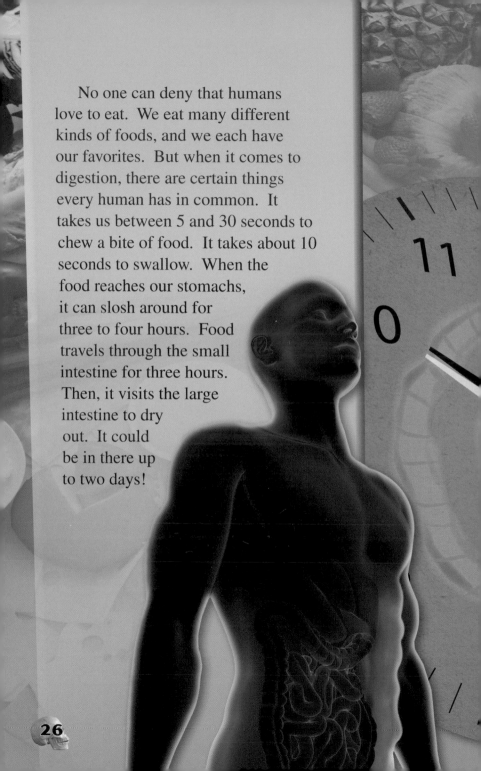

No one can deny that humans love to eat. We eat many different kinds of foods, and we each have our favorites. But when it comes to digestion, there are certain things every human has in common. It takes us between 5 and 30 seconds to chew a bite of food. It takes about 10 seconds to swallow. When the food reaches our stomachs, it can slosh around for three to four hours. Food travels through the small intestine for three hours. Then, it visits the large intestine to dry out. It could be in there up to two days!

Tick Tock

Food breaks down differently in our bodies. Some foods are hard to digest and others are easier, depending on the nutrients inside. Foods that are easier to digest pass through the body quickly. Foods that are harder to digest can spend time rotting in the intestine. It can take days before they become feces.

parsley

1 hour

blueberries

2 hours

broccoli

3 hours

brussels sprouts

4 hours

hamburger

more than 5 hours

DIG DEEPER!

The Truth About Toots

The bacteria in our intestines help us digest food. As they work, they create gas. Most people pass gas 14 times a day!

Most large farts are loud, but odorless. Smaller farts are quieter and smellier!

Farty Foods

beans

onions

fried foods

broccoli

turkey

soda

Gas can take up to 45 minutes to leave the body.

Burps move quickly.

Flatulence is a medical term for gas.

When gas leaves the body, it's a toasty 98.6° F.

If you could go into space without a suit and pass gas, it would have enough thrust to push you forward.

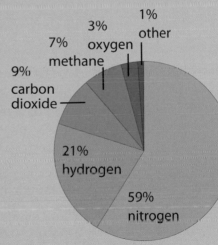

Gas Graph

The average toot is made up of these chemicals.

1% other

3% oxygen

7% methane

9% carbon dioxide

21% hydrogen

59% nitrogen

The chemicals that make gas smell make up less than 1 percent of each fart.

The Five Senses

It's hard to imagine life without our senses. They give us details about the world and help us survive. Sounds move in waves through air, water, and other objects. The outside of the ear directs sounds into the inner ear. Sound waves hit the ear—as long as they aren't filled with wax! The brain interprets the sound waves and tells us what we're hearing.

Clear that gunk out of your eyes! It's time to give the eyes a second look. Eyes collect information about the world. Light passes through the eye. The **retina** at the back of the eye absorbs the light. The brain makes sense of what the eyes see. Eyes are placed in the skull so we can see how far away things are. They help us watch baseball games, admire paintings, and see our families. Tears keep the eyes moist and healthy. Eyelashes protect the eyes from painful intruders like dust and sand.

Mixed Messages

People who experience **synesthesia** associate one sense with another. For example, they may hear a particular sound when they smell a rose. They might taste chocolate when they hear a violin play. Many associate a certain color with a specific number or letter.

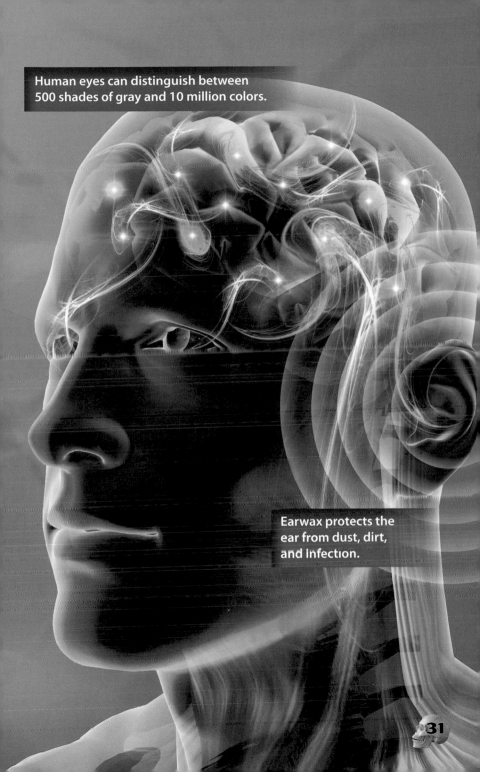

Human eyes can distinguish between 500 shades of gray and 10 million colors.

Earwax protects the ear from dust, dirt, and infection.

31

The human mouth can detect the flavor of foods, minerals, and poisons. Taste buds are arranged in patches on the top of the tongue. There are five basic tastes: sweet, bitter, sour, salty, and **umami** (oo-MAH-mee). *Umami* is a Japanese word that means "good taste." It is used to describe something that has a rich, long-lasting taste. Some cheeses, mushrooms, and meats have this taste.

Special cells inside the nose detect chemicals in the air. Those cells send messages to the brain. Smells can be good, like apple pie or pine trees. Or they can be bad, like rotting fish or skunk. Bad odors often warn of something that could cause disease.

You can feel the soft pillow against your face or the sharp rock underfoot thanks to nerve endings. Nerves in the skin detect **stimuli** (STIM-yuh-lahy) like heat, cold, or pressure. The nerve endings send a signal to the brain. These signals protect the body from danger.

The sense of taste is so dependent on the sense of smell that if you plugged your nose, you probably couldn't tell if you were biting into a crisp apple or a raw onion.

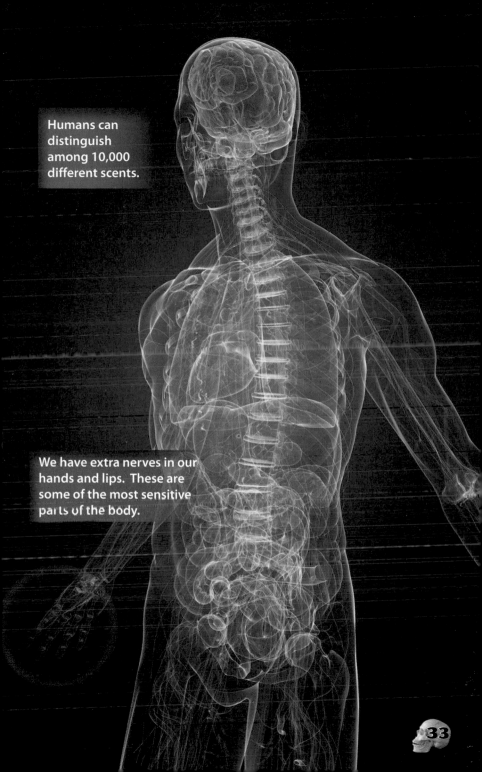

Humans can distinguish among 10,000 different scents.

We have extra nerves in our hands and lips. These are some of the most sensitive parts of the body.

33

Boggling the Brain

We depend on our senses to understand the world around us, and usually they don't deceive us. But once in a while, something goes wrong. Our senses can mislead us. They can trick us into believing something that isn't true.

Optical illusions are designed to fool your brain. Often, these tricks of the eye are based on the placement of objects in relation to one another. Look at the picture below. Are the red lines equal in size? The one on the right looks bigger, doesn't it? It's not. Your brain was tricked!

Falling Asleep

You are just about to drift off to dreamland when suddenly, you feel like you're falling and your body jerks awake. One theory is that this *hypnic jerk* happens when your muscles begin to relax. Perhaps the brain interprets this relaxation as a sign that you're falling and alerts your body to stay upright. Do you think that's what is meant by "falling" asleep?

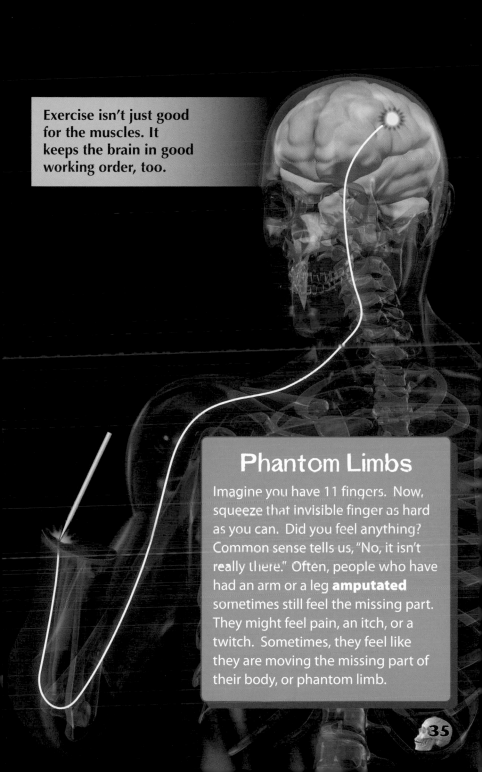

Exercise isn't just good for the muscles. It keeps the brain in good working order, too.

Phantom Limbs

Imagine you have 11 fingers. Now, squeeze that invisible finger as hard as you can. Did you feel anything? Common sense tells us, "No, it isn't really there." Often, people who have had an arm or a leg **amputated** sometimes still feel the missing part. They might feel pain, an itch, or a twitch. Sometimes, they feel like they are moving the missing part of their body, or phantom limb.

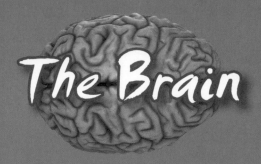

The Brain

Your brain does all the thinking. But have you done any thinking about the brain? The brain helps you remember phone numbers, and it knows how to make you talk and walk. The human brain invented computers and baseball. This is where our feelings, dreams, and new ideas come from.

The brain is the most complex part of our body. And it is the control center for everything else. This important organ receives information from the nerves. It also sends messages to other parts of your body. The brain monitors all the systems in the body. It keeps the body in a state of **homeostasis** (HOH-mee-uh-STEY-sis).

If you touch it, the brain feels like firm jelly.

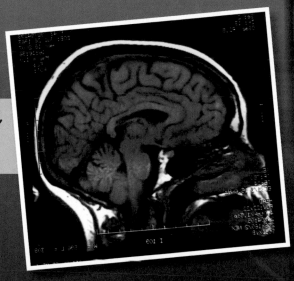

Ouch!

Modern doctors know the brain is fragile. In the past, the risks of brain surgery weren't as clear—but that didn't stop people from trying. Many ancient skulls have been found with holes in them. These brutal surgeries were used to treat headaches, epilepsy, and mental illness.

Some people say the brain looks gray. Others say it looks pink, green, or even blue!

Two Heads Are Better Than One

The human brain is made up of two **hemispheres** (HEM-i-sfeerz). Each side controls the opposite side of the body and is responsible for different types of thoughts. A thick band of nerves connects the two sides of the brain. This lets the hemispheres share information with each other.

The left side of the brain controls the right side of the body. This side of the brain helps us speak, make decisions, and analyze facts.

Left

If you are right-handed, you are mostly "left-brained."

"Left-brainers" are more often logical and focused on details.

Just as you are right-handed or left-handed, most people have one side of the brain that's stronger than the other.

The right side of the brain is good at hands-on activities, making art, and listening to music.

Right

If you're left-handed, you're most likely "right-brained."

"Right-brainers" are thought to be artistic and interested in big ideas.

Human Body 2.0

The human body has built giant cities, vehicles that can fly, and beautiful works of art. Humans have gone into space and traveled deep into the ocean. Our bodies let us lift enormous weights, feel amazing emotions, and have brilliant new ideas.

We have to travel great distances to explore new planets, but the study of gross anatomy allows us to view the strange landscapes of our own body's interior without going anywhere. We get the chance to see ourselves from the inside out—literally!

Every Part Works Together

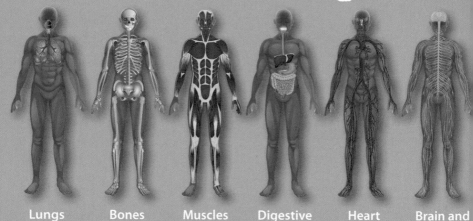

Lungs   Bones   Muscles   Digestive System   Heart   Brain and Nerves

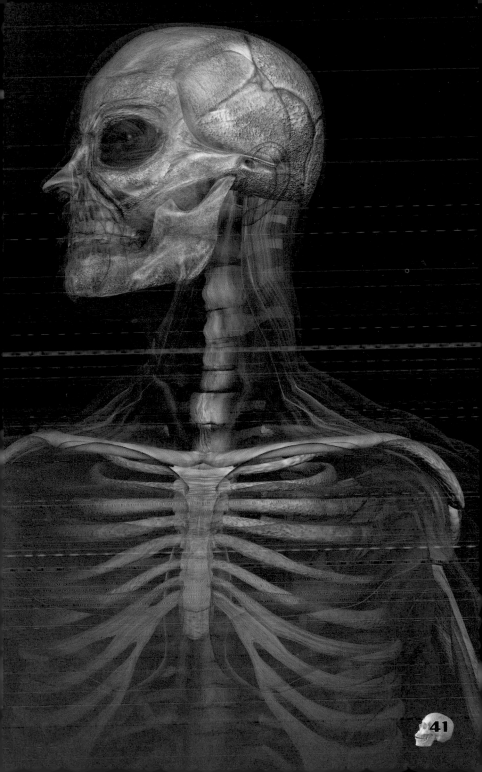

Glossary

amputated—cut off

bacteria—tiny one-celled life-forms

bloodletting—the practice of opening a vein and letting blood out in the hope of curing illnesses

cadavers—dead bodies dissected for study

calcium—a material that bones are made of

carbon dioxide—a waste product made by cells during respiration

cardiac muscle—special muscle that makes up the heart

cartilage—a firm, flexible type of connective tissue

circulatory system—the system of the body that includes the heart and blood vessels

deceased—no longer living

digestive system—the system of the body that breaks food into nutrients and waste

dissect—to cut open something to examine it

feces—solid waste that is eliminated from the body

glands—organs that secrete chemicals

hemispheres—half-sections of the brain

homeostasis—a state of stability when the body's systems are all working properly

ligaments—bands of tissues that connect bones or hold organs in place

microorganisms—very small living things that can only be seen with a microscope

nerves—cells that transmit signals to the brain or spinal cord

nutrients—elements necessary for life and health

organs—parts of the body that perform specific functions

oxygen—an element found in air that supports life

peristalsis—muscle contractions that move food through the digestive system

respiration—the act or process of breathing

retina—the area at the back of the inner eyeball that absorbs light

skeletal muscles—muscle tissues that are connected to the skeleton

smooth muscle—muscle tissue that contracts without voluntary control

sphincter muscles—ring-shaped smooth muscles that close a bodily opening

stimuli—events or things that cause a reaction from living things

synesthesia—a condition that includes a sensation (such as color) other than the one (such as sound) being stimulated

tendons—bands of tissue that connect muscles to bones

umami—a Japanese word used to describe one of the basic tastes that is rich and long lasting

Index

amputated, 35

bacteria, 14, 25, 28

blood, 4, 6, 17–23

bloodletting, 20

bones, 6–10, 12, 40

brain, 6, 30, 32, 34, 40

cadavers, 12–13

calcium, 8

carbon dioxide, 18, 20–21

cardiac muscle, 10

cartilage, 8

cells, 14, 18–21, 32

circulatory system, 20, 24

conjoined twins, 15

cough, 19

da Gama Bahia, Ricardo, 18

digestion, 24, 40

dissect, 12–13

doctors, 10, 12–13, 15, 20, 37

donation, 22 –23

ear, 30–31

earwax, 30 –31

elbow, 8

eye, 4, 10, 30–31, 34

face transplant, 16 –17

Father of Anatomy, 13

feces, 25, 27

flatulence, 29

foot binding, 9

gas, 4, 24, 28–29

glands, 14

hearing, 30

heart, 10, 20–21, 40

Herophilus, 13

intestine, 24–29

joints, 8

leeches, 20

ligaments, 8, 10

Little Hercules, 10

lungs, 18–21, 40

mammals, 6

microorganisms, 14

mouth, 18–19, 25, 32

muscles, 6, 10–12, 17, 34–35, 40

neck, 9

nerves, 17, 32–33, 36, 38, 40

nose, 14, 18, 32

nutrients, 20, 24–25, 27

optical illusions, 34

organs, 6, 14–15, 20, 36

oxygen, 18–21

Padaung, 9

peristalsis, 10

phantom limbs, 35

red blood cells, 19–20

red gold, 22

respiration, 18

retina, 30

saliva, 19, 25

Sandrak, Richard, 10

senses, 30, 34

skeletal muscles, 10–11

skeleton, 6, 8, 10, 12

skin, 5–6, 12, 14–15, 17, 32

skull, 7, 30, 37

smell, 29–30, 32

smooth muscle, 10

sounds, 30

sphincter muscles, 10

stomach, 10, 25–26

synesthesia, 30

taste, 30, 32

taste buds, 32

tendons, 8, 10

Thailand, 9

tongue, 32

touch, 36

transfusion, 22–23

waste, 10, 18, 25

Wiens, Dallas, 16

Bibliography

Daynes, Katie and Colin King. *See Inside Your Body.* **Usborne Books, 2006.**

Take a hands-on approach to learning. This lift-the-flap anatomy book follows the pathways of digestion and respiration.

Gould, Francesca. *Why You Shouldn't Eat Your Boogers and Other Useless or Gross Information About Your Body.* **Tarcher, 2008.**

Broken down by system, this book is full of awesome facts about human anatomy. Do *you* know how astronauts poop in space?

Green, Dan and Simon Basher. *Basher Science: Human Body: A Book with Guts.* **Kingfisher, 2011.**

Cells, DNA, bones, muscles, and other organs are all explained in colorful, memorable detail in this book.

Jankowski, Connie. *Investigating the Human Body.* **Teacher Created Materials, 2008.**

Find out what characteristics all seven billion humans on the planet share. This book explains how scientists study the human body.

More to Explore

Mutter Museum
http://www.collegeofphysicians.org/mutter-museum

This unusual medical museum includes preserved body parts such as Einstein's brain and exhibits on diseases and medicines.

Body Worlds: The Original Exhibition of Real Human Bodies
http://www.bodyworlds.com

These exhibitions include cross-sections of the human body and its parts using a process developed by Gunther von Hagens called *plastination*. The exhibit travels worldwide. Check out the schedule online to see if it will be visiting a city near you.

KidsHealth
http://kidshealth.org/kid

This site includes movies, games, recipes, and medical dictionaries that cover every major system in the body.

MEDtropolis: Home of the Virtual Body
http://www.medtropolis.com

This website is intended to educate kids and adults with the latest health information, including features like Health Calculators, Kids Health, and the Virtual Body.

About the Author

Timothy J. Bradley grew up near Boston, Massachusetts, and spent every spare minute drawing spaceships, robots, and dinosaurs. That was so much fun that he started writing and illustrating books about natural history and science fiction. He loves to create new creatures based on real bizarre animals. He also worked as a toy designer for Hasbro, Inc., and designed life-size dinosaurs for museum exhibits. As an artist, he has studied human anatomy for many years. Timothy lives in sunny Southern California with his wife and son.

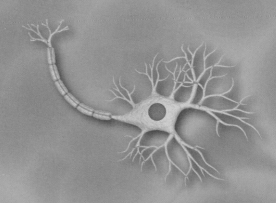